LAODICEA

LAODICEA

Eric Ekstrand

OMNIDAWN PUBLISHING
RICHMOND, CALIFORNIA
2015

Cover photo © Jennifer Ray, 2015, courtesy of the photographer

Cover Typefaces: Adobe Caslon Pro and Myriad Pro
Interior Typefaces: Adobe Caslon Pro, ITC Serif Gothic, and Myriad Pro

Cover and interior design by Gillian Olivia Blythe Hamel

Each Omnidawn author participates fully in the design of his or her
book, choosing cover art and approving cover and interior design.
Omnidawn strives to create books that align with each author's vision.

Offset printed in the United States
by Edwards Brothers Malloy, Ann Arbor, Michigan
On 55# Enviro Natural 100% Recycled 100% PCW
Acid Free Archival Quality FSC Certified Paper
with Rainbow FSC Certified Colored End Papers

Library of Congress Cataloging-in-Publication data

Ekstrand, Eric, 1984-
  [Poems. Selections]
  Laodicea / Eric Ekstrand.
      pages cm
  Includes bibliographical references.
  SBN 978-1-63243-003-8 (pbk. : alk. paper)
  I. Title.
  PS3605.K78A2 2015
  811'.6--dc23
                              2014040736

Published by Omnidawn Publishing, Richmond, California
www.omnidawn.com   (510) 237-5472   (800) 792-4957
10 9 8 7 6 5 4 3 2 1
ISBN: 978-1-63243-003-8

Plot:

a bitty lea
unpersuaded
by even He
who made it

Contents

9   Foreword
11   Acknowledgments

ONE

19   It Is Crucial to Be Able to Spot One
21   The Nemesis That Causes the Evening to Smudge
23   Janus
25   Every Aster as a Herald, Every Child a First Thing
28   No Crevice Is a Grimace, No Animal a Blended Thought
30   The Nemesis That Whiles Away,

TWO

35   The Extent of the Land
36   Travel
38   The Legend of the Musk Deer
44   Hannah's Strong Features
46   After WS Graham

THREE

51   An Exultet Roll
54   The Snake, in Medieval Emblem, Eats Its Tail,
           Then Eats Its Mouth
57   Corded, Metaled, Laurelled
59   Hedonic Tone Assessment

FOUR

65   A Few Creams
68   The Nemesis of Weekends
71   When Life Was Full, There Was No History
74   All Things From Eternity Are of Like Form and Come
           'Round in a Circle
80   The Nemesis of Fineness,
81   Laodicea

87   Notes

Foreword

> For I would that ye knew what great conflict I have for you,
> and *for* them at Laodicea, and *for* as many as have not seen
> my face in the flesh…
> —Colossians, 2:1

Coming to its senses and taking to the roads (you will recall Whitman's avowing himself as "afoot with my vision"), Vision relies more heavily, more lovingly upon devotion than it does upon courage. Devotion pays attention. Devotion has an eye for both here and hereafter. Truth be told, I am tired to death of courage. It is lauded everywhere; any new poet willing to risk an adjective or to torment a perfectly good noun into conjugations finds a hero's welcome somewhere in our paratactic spree. Find me a devoted poet. Find me a poem that both walks and stands its visionary ground. Such a poem will be competent to the conflicts of our day and, better still, to that eternal conflict of which Paul wrote so urgently to the Colossians.

Laodicea, in what is now Anatolia, was a metropolis of Empire on the margin of empire, and one of the centers of Early Christianity. Naturally, Saint Paul was concerned for his brethren there. Apocalyptically, Saint John of the Revelation had something very severe and, eventually, gorgeous in store for its women and men. In the new and nearer *Laodicea*, Eric Ekstrand sets his margins moving and finds a center everywhere his loving eye alights. Naturally, given the exigencies of our own bad empire, his concerns are tender and keen for flesh, for shrines in the flesh that undisguise the blasted shrines of these United States. Say the margin is a reindeer farm in North Carolina; say the center is "white tails / and little fur spirits rising from the anus." You get the picture. You also get, by way of devotion, an eros fighting the good fight, a freedom as wild as prophecy any time, here and hereafter. And then say further, apocalypse is in the air…hell, apocalypse *is* the air anymore hereabouts.

> …There is
> Endless permission

And no supporting structure.
It is not a house

So much as a marina
Of Mars-orange light where

Every person is an almost-entity
Or the mention of a person.
("Nemesis of Weekends")

Yet Ekstrand's devotion to disasters revealed and reviled proves disaster gorgeous in good time: "Offshoot of silence / In the backyard // And a melon-colored bird." Here is a poet of original endurance given to conflict and given always also to aftermath. You've got to hand it to Saint John; he took the whole trip. And it is a fullest pleasure to hand a troubled moment of American poetry to this *Laodicea*. The poems here are fresh to sustain the visions they avow.

And unto the angel of the church of the Laodiceans write;
These things saith the Amen, the faithful and true witness…
—Revelation 3:14

Donald Revell

Acknowledgments

Poems in this book have appeared previously in journals and magazines, sometimes in different forms and under different titles:

Catch Up: "The Nemesis of Weekends"; "The Nemesis That Causes the Evening to Smudge"

Indiana Review: "When Life Was Full, There Was No History"

jubilat: "It Is Crucial to Be Able to Spot One"

Oversound: "Corded, Metaled, Laurelled"; "Janus"; "Laodicea"; "The Snake, in Medieval Emblem, Eats Its Tail, then Eats Its Mouth"

Poetry: "A Few Creams"

I'd like to make grateful acknowledgment to the editors of these magazines, especially to Christian Wiman, Fred Sasaki and Valerie Johnson, with whom I was fortunate to work when I was very young and who, along with Don Share, have supported my work throughout the years, to the Ruth Lilly estate and to the Poetry Foundation, whose financial support helped me to write and finish my degree.

I'd like to thank all of my teachers, especially: Gesh Spiegel, Jennifer LaGarde, Mary Beth Ferrell, Dean Franco, Evie Schockley, Conor O'Callaghan, Vona Groarke, Jane Mead, Tony Hoagland, Mark Doty, Martha Serpas, Jim Zebroski, Tamara Fish, Bruce Smith, and Dr. Maya Angelou. Thanks also to Lynn Voskuil, boldface: a conference for emerging writers, j. Kastely, and to all of my students.

I'd like to thank Inprint! Houston (my friends and neighbors), and the Brown Foundation, Inc., for their financial support. Gratitude also to the University of Houston Department of English and Creative Writing Program and Writers in the Schools Houston, especially: Robin, Long and Jack. Thanks also to *Gulf Coast: A Journal of Literature and Fine Arts*, and to the Sewanee Writers' Conference, especially: Mark Strand, Michael Dumanis, Kimberly Johnson, Mark Jarman, and Claudia Emerson.

Gratitude to my friends and colleagues who challenge me and are so kind: Sean Bishop, Sam Amadon, Liz Countryman, Hannah Gamble, Patrick Lucy, Eric Kocher, Laura Eve Engel, Laurie Cedilnik, Glenn Shaheen, Michael West, the Wake Forest University Department of English, Wake Forest University Press, and the Writing Program at Wake Forest University, especially: Anne Boyle, Ryan Shirey, Aimee Mepham, Elisabeth Whitehead, Eric Stottlemyer, Phoebe Zerwick, Jimmy Butts, Laura Aull, Zak Lancaster, Laura Giovanelli, and Erin Branch. Thanks also to Tom Phillips for his good faith and counsel.

Gratitude to my friends: Todd, Karl, Carol, Laura, Callie, Alex and Cat French, Geoffrey, Bethany and Rob Welborn, Charlene, Matty, Raymie, Chris and Kendra Plating, Amy, Benjamin, and John.

Thanks especially to Jennifer Ray, my long-time friend who generously provided the cover art for this book.

Lastly, I'd like to thank my parents for their patience and support during many uncertain years, and Danny for his cheerful love.

The Antients used to sacrifice to the Goddess Nemesis; a Deity who was thought to look with an invidious Eye on human Felicity, and to have a Delight in overturning it.

H. FIELDING

ONE

It Is Crucial to Be Able to Spot One

A nemesis is not quite
An animal, it is the premise
Of an animal where nothing

Is fullform. If you have here

And here a nemesis,
Then you have two frames
Over which the total lusts

And bodies of animals

Have almost been laid.
They enter rooms
As inexactly as anxieties

Or children. It is much more

Like a nemesis that the ancients
Chiseled there every abstract
Polyp on totems and every

Generalized hair.

A nemesis has genitals
Like the approximate
Genitals of prepubescents

In their nightclothes. Nemeses'

Underdemonstrated legs—
If the chief merit of language
Is clearness, their movements

Are difficult

To find, limber as dusks.
What could be more
Indistinct than fur?

The nemeses have found

A way. Their pounds
Are in the woods among
Their meals. The hoop

Of the anus, it is a sorrowful

Feeling. Hard to say
What kind of butcher
It would take to carve one.

If you hear its sounds,

They might be sounds
From other places
And in what way, precisely,

Have they been misconstrued?

Is it like how the skin
Was misconstrued as pink
Or gray? Their corners get lost

In the eye, but

What I'm sure of is
How much more alike
One is to men's suppressions.

This man's.

The Nemesis That Causes the Evening to Smudge

Is named Nicholas
Very clearly. Nicholas
Takes many liberties

All of which are seen
When there is no polarity
In the sky.

Nick is great at parties.
You could think of Nick
As a virgule as well

As you could the sky
An interpenetration. The way
Evenings are described

As "secretory" or "lavender"
Or "chemesized" all refer
To techniques established

By Nick, by which he means
For the audience to ask,
What is being lost and what

Gained—or else, what is surviving?
This is just one
Of the challenges Nick

Presents. When he imitates
The derangements
Outsiders have

By way of his evenings, is he taking
Advantage of them?
Sun, the elder strawberry mark,

Is heraldic, down,
And roughened. Rubefacient
Is it hewn making

All the world a rubberneck
Passing. Nick is accidental
When he yells at his mother.

He is always trying to be tragic
And the ascension/descension
Of every visiting thought

He calls a game of snakes
And ladders. In his work,
There is very little thrift or peace.

It is entirely cosmetic,
Which is another way of saying,
It is a mirror of a life lived

Among people. That he is an agent
Of sexual dexterity is a fact
Proven through his skies'

Fanlike and nonmaterial shrines
To pinks and the desirous
Thistles of women.

When you ask him,
Women's thistles? He says,
Only because there aren't many

Things that have more "vivre."
Every night, his work makes
Its own retort like a lid.

Janus

1

Wooden panels painted
with historical events
(and this one especially
where the gear of war grinds)
above the glass vase,
whose inward curves operate
as self-pity, holding roses—
those jelly-remarking hearts
and communist gatherings
in night forests
where universal love
is most secret—
are the department chair's prize.

We are all too young
to be here;
so we go and have a real drink
in off-hand catchiness
shaping our lives
into mythical good or bad.

This is the golden year
of the rock-and-roll memoir

and everyone at the table
has a different thing
they are trying to make happen.
A prepared sound.
Another prepared sound.
If there are two shadows
for one object,
there are two lights.

2

The word "culture"
itself doesn't seem to exist.
It is like a Janus
that is always
looking at you
at the same time
it looks away
from the corners of either
one of two
sets of eyes.
When you try to meet
one set
they look away
and the other set instantly
looks at you
and you try to meet them
and they look away. Then,

you look at the place
where the two
faces join
and just *stare* at it,

because it's the weirdest
part of the whole thing.
But, still, you feel
on familiar ground
because it is an archetype.
This is the first
moment of welcome
you've had in weeks.

Every Aster as a Herald, Every Child a First Thing

To begin with,
there is a landscape

with intervals of wind
collectors that are angels

with turbines. This suggests
the divinity of man. Imagine it:

a real landscape that one
could throw rocks into.

There is some action
of the landscape by which

it is known. Knowing it
is the action of the landscape.

Minds are turbines.
The landscape is a semipermeable

membrane that minds
churn rocks into.

More importantly, this is an actual
landscape unlike any you have known

with a long list
of colors and materials

and there are little rips
in it from the rocks. There is

this effect of vibrancy.
There is an artery

in the landscape that is a stream
to be actually and just a stream

or the stream's effect.
The landscape thrums

like the aftermath of a struck harp.
It is simple lumber.

The earth's rug landscape
thrown over a green spot.

It is a fur.
It is peeling gilt.

It could be mistaken to sleep
and is mown.

Alighted on by numbers of.
The landscape is protective

of the thing that grows it.
The landscape is called out to.

It is a hibiscus and a climate.
It is the length of a religion.

It is very hard and wooden.
Children of the earth

are drinking tall boys
and worrying about money

in its glades of forsythia.
They love each other deep

in the gelatin of their eyes.
Their love is a small concert.

It is sometimes dishonest.

Summer cave of empty green-black,

you are the Buddha that makes
me saddest of all.

No Crevice Is a Grimace, No Animal a Blended Thought

A part of it is neglect
and a part is hiddenness

that the landscape
is missed because of.

It is an original startling.
The landscape is the original

landscape whose being missed
allows ambition to go on

with every man and then me.
The stimulated pattern

of red pocks on white
lilies sensitive close

to the center and light-
blue leaves repeat for balance

below the lilies that droop
like half-peeled swans

and can only tell about themselves.
All flowers are narcissus

but it isn't negative the way
we usually see it.

The landscape is a lawny
crèche. Ambition has patterns

of missing the landscape—
ten o' clock five coat buttons—

which, because they are patterns,
can never be effortless exactly.

To take a complete account
would injure the landscape

into shyness
ants go underground

beyond the creek of rural,
southern childhood before

the sky's religious blue.
There is no remorse

in the landscape and no joy,
just regular effulgence

how we are supposed to live.
The cardinal has sleekness

that is science fiction
with its twelve-tone-scale throat.

A black woman walks by.
Depression causes blindness.

All the mallards look like
decoys on a desk.

The Nemesis That Whiles Away,

Luxuriant in his products,
Does his dwindling

And produces nothing
Vain. It is a restful peach

That he leaves in place
Of himself on a hammock

Or a hillock or among
Straws and drinks

And he twists from out
Of himself the peach

That is luxuriant and without
Vanity. No one thinks

To ask where he's gone
Beyond the peach because

The peach is so transfixing
And is sometimes laid next to

The Nemesis that Whiles with Him
And she has left a red pear.

TWO

The Extent of the Land

For Danny

North Carolina has land
even still, super-abundant. Believe it.

Pert scrapes of bushes and this reindeer
farm with two reindeer, which are later
discovered to be _____ deer,

I forget, shaggier than white tails
and little fur spirits rising from the anus

these have not. It is the quietest,
and behind the deer

is the black, Shinto representative
of the deer. It looks like spruce.
My boyfriend is in the car.

What is his representative? How black and how huge?
It being the fear of this protector

through which my protector
seems to love him.

Travel

On the wallpaper
behind me, lotuses

sit like white ladies
sit for yoga at the Y

—unsuppressed.
On the facing wall

is a mural of a bamboo
forest that looks

exactly how I expect
a bamboo forest to look.

In a clearing
are pandas: six

simultaneously.
They are eating near

a generalissimo.
Maybe they are

his resurrected grandfathers.
I am between the two walls

and point out a fish in the tank
that keeps floating

near the light box.
The little flowers on the table

are white piths, entire lives.
He doesn't look up.

The fish is a stalled-out
tug in the middle

of her comrades
who are golden barges, constantly

fanning their imperial oars.
It doesn't seem right,

exactly, to say in the vagueness
of a drink, *Acute* Alcoholism.

He was right there
in front of me and somewhere

else, perhaps
in a very beautiful country.

The Legend of the Musk Deer

Musk Deer, in his
toffee purposelessness,
lead a generally direct

life of leg gestures
content among

the greenhearts
of the forest until,
once, he smelled

an odor, beautiful, drift
from beyond the compass

of his deer mind
and became bound
by the thought

he might possess its source
and so bounded day and night

between every thing that grew:
lilliputian violets, avocado,
roses' satire, behind the roses

flax, seclusionist sage plants,
daffodils' shockability,

first rites plum vines,
musty inner of a haystack,
mostly flowers, though,
reaching out
of himself into the condensed

heart instructions
of flowers, into the crucial

small theater-spaces,
the sex comedies of flowers,

the unenforced
law and eyestrain, the unplanned

sameness and secret inducement
of flowers, into
the disarmored breast

of a field of flowers, greenery
and so-on under
the rosy-fingered dawn,

the light-understanding paintwater,
the self-immolation yellow and orange
of flowers, into spiritual hangouts
of flowers, the votive

and indifferent life-function
of survival flowerage,
into meadowsweet rituals, on

and on until he became
old in his circulations

and collapsed with fatigued
springmood in a boundary

of jonquil, tusk pierced
his side with his overdone

old war horn weight
as he fell, releasing
the odor, mockingly

more potent,
that he had discriminated

every forest-part grasping
at, years, and died weeping
not for his injury.

This will be a poem
about how parties are like that.

Parties like this one where
Hannah, in her shift

skirt patterns, considers
a barrette, smoothing

down her hair
over the thought

of a boyfriend. She
smoothes her
hair and it is just

hair now with
nothing else. This

is how loneliness
works. I see you,
Hannah. You and I

are similar germs.
Two laughs develop
arm-in-arm down

the stairs. Hannah
smoothes her cheek

and becomes
a slope of the couch

while the plush girls,
florid, leave fulsome

in the rudiment
of their drunkenness,

which is good
and basically clean.

How unsafe
the clear light
of chandeliers

where Hannah curls is.

Now it's Pete.
There goes Pete.

People can move
as if they were,

themselves, chatter.

Hannah, when I see
how you give the barrette
a troubled soul,

I become an animist.

The talents
of the night shine

in the sky and two
semi-beers are combined

that no one drinks.
A light weakens
only the *physical*

shadows about Hannah
and alike is the upstairs

table of blemishless
friends who fall
in temporary love

joking to each other
in self-conscious half-truths.

Into night-happening
sadness everyone dances

holding themselves
in readiness or incentives

of genitals or in disgorging
among the dramaturgy

and nonresonant killings
of rap music confidence
or among the Blue Ridge

Mountains where no one
can be implicated.

It is true that the world
is awful and it is also true

that an orange gives itself totally.
For Hannah's wiggling,

there is a Harvard-Yale
race vying: Harvard

is Sean and Yale
is a guy I don't know.
I do actually love Sean.

Hannah, come here by me
in your natural

quality on the stairs—
so that I can say,
"You are the first person
I've known,
who by continuing to be fragile

her whole life, isn't."

Hannah's Strong Features

I have been here
at the fake Parthenon
in Nashville
because we both love it:
large pagan repeat
in that concrete
insuspended with manila pebbles
that every imitation Bauhaus
building was made of in the seventies.
I'm writing to you
about our friendship
for which I am offering,
as a metaphor,
the Nashville Parthenon,
because it is hilarious, large
and sad.
Only, please, read
its purposelessness and dimensions
from your body.

You were always wearing
gladiator sandals,
which I know are a Roman reference.
This place
and those shoes say something
about your confused power.

I'm looking at it now
as a weird, gigantic
kid is pinwheeling wildly
and at intervals growls
a "ba" that ruptures into
a vulturic screech arriving

full-speed to then punch
his mother directly
in the ass. She is angry

suppressing to not have any attention
additionally drawn there,

which is like the unsaid things
between us. Hannah, I am
indwelled by two gods:
Compulsion and Compulsion,

which your subversiveness
thinks is great and which, to me,
when they are ruling
dually, feels only hectic.

Imagine a routine
panegyric that has finally
come to the point on its steps

held forth by some delegate haranguer
of the ancient world. Anything

can seem important when
it's done in front of the Parthenon.

Our friendship
is like a commonwealth
with its grapeshot

system of competing interests
idiotically expanding
then abruptly consolidated

as a single building
of unity, symmetry and contemplated
whiteness—necessary
if only as an overlordish hope.

After WS Graham

It does not matter who you are,
it does not matter who I am.

This book has not been purposely
made for any reason.

It has made itself by circumstances.
It is aimed at nobody at all.

It is prenumerated
like a columbarium that has spaces

to fill reverently
waiting one two three four,

you know, five, old song
up to eighty-something

little kindergarten cubbies
with perfect slate plates which are complete

life boxes. What happens
in the book—there isn't more to say,

"What happens in the book."
It is self-actualization like you

have to select one of the eggs.
It amounts to the whole

casual person who accounts for himself.
We were in Chicago

in February at the multifaceted Wrigley—
a building that, like a friend,

walks beside you as you turn
the corner. We were only there for a moment:

stops of air, the sleeze
of old snow. We watched the street salters

burn north yellow
turned around before Southside

because the poor don't pay enough in taxes
from the muffle of a lobby

we ducked into. This and every memory
will be folded away, Sean,

and I am already forgetting it.
I don't mean to alarm you,

I'm just telling you the facts.
Someone will sell your things.

The objects will tilt with their new context.
Even when the whole thing

is done, nothing has been
made to happen that counts

commemorated
by a slate plaque that gives the dates

for how it took time for night
to look exactly like the day.

THREE

From the Early Life of Harold Hayes,
Editor and Author

An Exultet Roll

Wake Forest, NC 1948

They come bumping
out of the student hall,

the avoidance of racism
ruddering sleekly
through their talk.
There is no interruption;

the scene
is a unified
field, a procedure
of the land: curseless,
undergraduate, and completely hot.

The athletic sweaters are wrestled
out of and whipped across

single shoulders, grappling
in the sudden uniformity
of disuse, creaturely and dank.

Protuberances in spring
and most pert trimmed bushes
extended and perpendicular
the okra-seeming
buds of daylilies thrum
predictively with renovation.
One class above Ammons,
who might be excluded
somewhere.

White, remorseless
wealth, uncarefully interested
in jazz. Even the disorder
is wholesome and every body

is a healthy body
of the kind reserved
in heaven. With allowance,
the dogwoods; with hilarity, the forsythia;

with grounding
resolve, the rhododendron.

It is as though because
the Baptists are educating,

the Lord shows forth His pleasure and His pleasure
is yellow, white and deep green.

The boys, strong
in unpresuming post-war
builds, are so sexy
they are creative. Rounding
the library,
the outside pressurizes
supramundane, relieved in skill
by open sky. The field house,
racketed and pegged, in the histaminic distance

now with all the powers of the other world—
laughing, centering—draws close
over their huge erections.

Nautical reference
runs through the clothes.

Hanging around the buildings
every girl imprecise in her lightness
and she blendeth; where,

rested at her earthly spot,
she knows that every word
has its ancestor,
What is that called and what is that called?

It bunkered there, if it did,
warming the solarplexi

of the medieval: the little refusing
soul, guardant only
in the post-positive

when all human accounts
are settled and we have arced
hugely into the last world.

Why, when it has been
so thoroughly replaced,

remediate to its preemie
mysterium? *Bath qol*
strong-armed, usually,
in the translation
as *voice of God* means
Daughter of a Sound or

for Elijah he called it *a sound
of sheer silence.*

A white motor boat
noses at the shore
called "Daughter
of a Sound." The boat
isn't particularly permanent;

although there's the sense
that no one certain put it there
and no one, likely,
is soon to take it up.

The Snake, in Medieval Emblem, Eats Its Tail, Then Eats Its Mouth

Winston-Salem, NC 1935

It is unconsolidated orderliness
that, an acre from the curb,
sun porch on either side,

the Stratford Road colonial
licenses: white boards,

orange brick, Kelly green.
His mother's interior architecture makes
his culture in the earliest
so that he starts to be intersectional,

which is the beginning of,
among more positive impulses,
sheer embarrassment.
Like, the first time on the phone,
coached by his mother,
he has to talk to his friend's mother
is sexually confusing.

In the anti-Enlightenment big
dining room at home
the religious adamancy is cellular.

Heavy gold brocade curtain,
drawn sheers of rough-hewn cotton,
very modern cross-hatching,
enamel ashtrays, curvaceous chairs'
deep, resistant tufting.

It is reverent that adults bend
down to correct Harry.

Behind the house,
the aculture of trees'
frightening openness and a system

of creeks ordered through pipes
under the streets are, together, another
world that can be dropped into

eagerly, young, of ancient, unresisted sadness,
close lesson,
and cool dark green.

All of the extremity has turned in
for Harry:

unpreventable, he's unpreventable
behind a shield
suggested by a bent elbow.
It's not only that there's
a dragon in his mind, or his friend's mind—

composite of cigarettes and viperous
plantlife—but, also, can you really say
where Harry is or ever is?
The frog that changes
in the dirt's a theme.

The friend's house
the road takes out from,
ordered on either side
after pick-up

with white petite forests
as the servants to greet them

in an upstairs downstairs
melodrama, that Harry
and his mother leave, become

more brown-golden.
The road

never strikes out into a field
or turns.

A gray and orange bird
is the only emissary
from the interior.

The two characters:
one is a closed prayer book
and one is a closed hymnal.
Or better,
one is a closed hymnal
and one is his father.

Corded, Metaled, Laurelled

Reynolds Building, Winston-Salem, NC 1936

The stacked, New Deal
limestone opens
at intervals in iron

deco windows
rhomboid

arrow feather trim
a brass, rotating door,
less casual era
and when it came

to social immediacy,
more brutal: the exhibits

of stylized
industry the twenties

flaunted when decoration
mimicked necessity—

then, men did not type.
The employee cafeteria
muralized gold and red
and green and copper,

radiating composition
and pastel Gatsby-ites
in Byzantine length showing
disaffection amid feline
smoke was converted

on Holy Saturday
for the humanitarian

distribution of live chicks
to area children
dyed in psychotropic neons:
sickened and jittery
imagination fluff.

That on Easter afternoon
they would be swept
into dustpans

poisoned from the dye
was not part of this joy,

because the chicks
were seen at the angle
of paschal mystery

where death was present,
but ignored.

Hedonic Tone Assessment

Wilkes County, NC 1901

To be a Hayes in Purlear
is to be thorough.
The town, itself,
is a deficit

and New Hope Baptist Church.
They don't beg, which is one way
embarrassment can look like virtue.

Every house is hindered white,
contrived directly

on the dirt
with no mediary bush to the lot.

The women don't look
any particular way.

Church is out
and there is a whole week left.
Where the father is very busy,
James reads some.

The factory lace
is brown at the bottom

from the radiator
and some kind of flat,
shield-shaped beetle
slowly proliferates in the blinds,
three.

It is possible to use loneliness
as echolocation.
The guttering out of a woman's
deep voice has an audience
even if it's just James.

Theft at Furches'
Evergreen Warehouse in West Jefferson;
Desirable Black Mountain Subdivision
Burns. Purlear must borrow
its news. The garden's pepperminty

where unsurity
stays out as pure unsurity
green as pure green.

FOUR

A Few Creams

The spine is a slide
of human marvels;

it is a hierarchy of white

florets; it is a cult
of secret brothers;

it is a deliberate

list. So, look
how the spineless

relax in their

unblushing banality.
I lose my patience

in Winston where

no discoveries
are ever made

and the only

inner lavishment
is the bar, occasionally.

The spineless aspire

to incessant interludes
that never arrive

anywhere and that can't

remember wherefrom
they came. She is slightly

spineless, for instance:

her dress is
cream her skin

is cream her

creamy mind is fine
and her life will

end finely—how sad

is that to think of,
the finery of a cream

life? It is the saddest

of all truths that
can be read on

a person's face

in a decorous garden
that person has planted

themselves and of which

they are explaining
to you the intricacies

and expense: "notice how

in the light," "three
pallets shipped

last week," "have complementary

attitudes when it comes
to soil type

and moisture." She

isn't wicked; but, also,
she destroys the art of her life.

The Nemesis of Weekends

Monday through Friday
In lighterage reports

Or the garlic presses
Of kitchen sink

Dramas or the finchy
Women at the desks

Or the linsey-woolsey
Problem in the bed,

A discontent
Back-and-forth

Is the Nemesis of Unlinked
Home and Work. But we will

Look at the Nemesis
Of Weekends. Lissome

The mother and the sheets
Are indistinct in their line

Of retreat into the day.
Gregory, this nemesis, has braceleted

The mother and father
Together in the Saturday

That lapses to Monday
And is a kind of mezzanine

Or midfield. Philter
Of lunch on the porch,

Peppered tomatoes.
The father's microgravity

Of beer and sexual longing
Lead him, incomplete, in circles

Around the Saturday
As a cloud-appearance, not really

Furthered at all. There is
Endless permission

And no supporting structure.
It is not a house

So much as a marina
Of Mars-orange light where

Every person is an almost-entity
Or the mention of a person.

For a minute, something
Comes into focus:

The open texture
Of a glass vase

And the polyrhythm of blue
And white tile among which the mother

Intended to make a joke, that's all.
There is fruit

And wood around
The remediless joke and a little

Offshoot of silence
In the backyard

And a melon-colored bird.
Newfangled means "worded"

As in "of the fang." New, here,
Means "unfamiliar"—it was

Hard to recognize
The mother in the words,

Which were the publication
Of some old pre-thought.

The riverscape Saturday
Or the airy church architecture

Saturday or the father's
Brown study Saturday

Were not in sequence
With the other days, but

Were stopgaps with no sense of what
Was previous or will be next.

When Life Was Full, There Was No History

Into enclosures, crosshatched,
the modernization mornings

do is spent.

Over the warp
and emphasis of their dreams,

off-seasoners unselectively

shift like regional
pronunciation or waves

whose complex sounds,

rounded by the distance
from the hotel

(he curves up in bed)

are the understated
cross-purposes around

which Wilmington is summoned

(barely sophisticated
marshland a few resorts caused),

caused constantly, sleeping.

He curves up in bed,
the sliding door

is open, his back

is light blue,
and it is ridicule

of the ocean to live there.

Nothing can be built.
Every house is just suggested

by the temporary

emotion, "stilts";
and, anyway, we haven't fully

begun yet to live by

the shifts last century
in the quantum understandings

of time and space

that would cause us
to actually *perceive* the beach house

as more sievelike

or bendable or
as whatever metaphor

the popular science writers

would furnish
or as the wind

in medieval Japanese

ink drawings.
I imagine

that life would be more

complex and also rounded
by distance. The mind and the world

together are a Co-Cathedral;
so, don't worry, lay down.

All Things from Eternity are of Like Form and Come 'Round in a Circle

1

Daily, overthrowing Nashville, racist
otherwise but kind, has given

that it's not important any longer neither
that Lucinda Williams, Loretta Lynn, nor

any woman, they should cross their legs when,
seated, play guitar—delight in the Lord—

so there's something less of fear in the world than there was.
The loss of weight Lucinda's voice is meeting

into ranges of what people call the "Twenty-first Century,"
I call "Nashville." People under rolled steel

joists drinking become more
smooth-mannered, long,

within their overdrawn bank accounts
and the newly-minted washboard the opener's

brought on again as a tiny rectangle of broken ground
to sing around for its funniness that over

time becomes frank but is never able to be vulnerable,
unlike even the drums, is combed

with his nickel picks. Intelligent stage lights—
distortion of the face and body—are an orrery

during which a lamp is put in place of the sun.
Disinterest, that old home, becomes

a kind of calmness: people mimicking talking
in a happy medium of temperance, justice, and assuagement

while the sexy plantswoman sells tamales on Nodose.
She is almost pottery and the boyfriends

of extensile Belmont girls, who say they might
go hottubbing later with choice fatigue, kiss

each other on the mouth. Humankind can't
bear much goodness even though they say they want it:

the routine for everyone
for which the dumb, American idea

of nonconformity no room is given.
To say that, "the meeting place of divergent   .

attitudes—Lucinda—that there is no safety device
for is kept tonight in jungle green seaboard

pants of which the corporate worship
is wholehearted, she having made the letter-

perfect choice to cover Springsteen before
a crowd of peopled smartphones" is pretty

much the whole thing. Take the chromey resonator
on the dobro that is the canning factory

of songs as well as fiddles, the compassionate
conservatives of songs—

in between Lucinda intuits
the valance or the seat of feelings,

but she is an ordinary woman.
In between, she is black

as The Myth of The Bird in the Hall
is mostly black.

2

Before the show, there were lacrosse players
ending practice on the field other side

of the street who read as an op-ed
column on man-powered weapons. For,

or against? For. And I am also
for, overthrown by the cuirasses they wear

and the marlinspikes with which they battle
their unfeeling homelives. After

the show, the mink farm of hispid words
is the concert-goer's drunken mouth, where its curry

smells and cusses only are the brainwork. Beautiful
she sits in her boxpleats aloud. Flamboyant,

we forget, was an actual architectural
style, where Apple Inc. can't stand

euphuism even as it answers from angels' ancestral
positives: the porticos at the church of St. Maclou,

the transept of Senlis. Now, imagine
if a cathedral became interactive on Jameson,

optimum jutting, and you'll know
what her conscience-stricken friends

were trying to convince to go home.
If they could know her mind, they'd see it lying

inside her yelling on a bed of black,
forgetful pasture grass, if not enlightened,

then at peace beyond all thinking.

3

During soundcheck—before even the Lacrosse
players—the music critic could hear roadwork

caballeros singing among the forklifts:

> *Lucifer, I see you brother*
> *Hanging in the morning laughter*
> *Like a pupil in the day.*

> *Lucifer, your eyes forthright*
> *Of every murder in the bible:*
> *Set rhinestones in the day.*

> *Lucifer, the blue-black packet—*
> *Soaked plum, your heart—*
> *Purses deadly in the day.*

Around him, the giant cop-out
season finesses into the park below the tour bus

preparing for substitution by girlish spring
resigned as an internal auditor for Boeing Corp.

In the critic's mind, fraudulency-reason
forfeits the direct forgiveness earthly things

have for him in extravaganza—engaged violet,
heavy-hearted cake, player pianos' figments.

Recall the palmy days of Clinton-era Nashville
with its orderly lesbians and most things store-bought.

4

The pure North Star, Lucinda, is glamorized

as a glass harmonica free. No, the award moon,
Lucinda, is cheval glass at the audience's pleasure,

reflecting, who rejects heartbreak itself (sloppy
people) but requests bearable songs of heartbreak

to talk over, lingual strings, the tenor sounds
of which recur as the insubstantial hum of wants

ten-thousand, a hundred-thousand one into
the other in fluency that lives their days

for them at the club on Barcado, that presses
against unknowns, the first smoke of creation,

like anything else does and is filled with douchebags.
It makes loneliness, the second smoke that makes

the cosmic mother hold the cosmic error angry below
her tit, which is the third smoke of creation, the fourth

smoke is anxiety and the fifth is the child error
stomping off alone into the desert mountains.

5

In the pictures the next day, the audience
tags the stewey-eyes of early humanity they've posted

subtley cross that *this* is the expected thing.
The morning is commonly sad like the sad naturalness

animals keep for us without ambition and differs with me
about the fact of its sadness. The morning says,

"What can you say for sure? You're still drunk."
"Morning, I say you're handsome and a golden

jubilee caught in the worldly touch of waking up—
the ghostly presence of every ever morning."

The morning lounges prehistoric on the morning's
coronation thrones. It is a fresh institutional

revision, a change in the hiring structure,
                                        generally a new day.

The Nemesis of Fineness,

Pulchit, in crewneck methyl violet
Makes imaginary worlds basic in her form.
She has a new sweater that's well-turned.

It is a phrase that she takes on
And off throughout the day—the phrase,
"I'm ready" or its variant, "I'm not ready"—

With gentle handling. She confronts
Her want, migrating dune, as much as
A rational materialist can, mostly

By "reorienting priorities." The standard-
Bearer of the violet sweatercade that
Wastes through Nordstrom together in a line,

Called sometimes the "Nemesis of Drinking
Saltwater," she is represented by the ancients
As a squiggle, which is water, and a spear

Of wheat that means, "craving" or "regeneration."

Laodicea

That I can't have You, rival
to personal choice, completely

without dying as the president's
helicopters in trinity

for confusion fly low
over the river, conspiracy

black as You are
conspiracy black in low, stern

minerals, is one unconscious
consternation I have kept, Land.

Gripped-down plants
sprung in middle-states

are slightly more
like us to You and slightly

more like You to us. People
can only think of the plants as objects

of beauty or use. In Washington,
all of the plants are protestant,

mid-Atlantic, small and old
like oldest mountains are smallest.

Like Larkin-darkened post-war
Britain, the old mountains
Are concise and Lenten;
Or like Auden (if I were sarcastic
Because they are wrinkled
And in America). But with
Auden, I'm not sarcastic.
He is a great small mountain.
These have been my two simple elegies.

Smallest tear drop leaves
in republican hunter green,

green chair leather
tightened with brass, so that a bush

looks like something a campaign
analyst might strategize upon.

The golden dog pauses
valueless among the muscle

of the word rhododendron.
A little triangular garden

below an equestrian north
of Dupont, west of Adams Morgan

is a leniency city architects
permit You to mark the small

difference between fashionable
young, the rich homosexuals

and a famous Russian restaurant.
The horse strides nobly

towards the edge of an iron block
in preemptive slapstick;

except, if You've actually seen
a horse fall (You must've)

You know it isn't funny.
Constant, anonymous grass

and a decorative black iron gate
are all unhurried. A bit of

"The Wound Dresser" above
the metro entrance is a chilling

way to go underground.
This has been my third simple elegy.

Before the Duke Ellington Bridge
going west on the right

is a plaster finial above the door post
of a row house on which

are cast two ladies gathered
in Elysian roaches repainted:

one as a Greek woman and one
as a black woman of post-social-reform

anachronism, meringued
in olive branches—a refashion

intent unlike the Elysian Fields, Land,
or the baby panda that rolls over

virtual in the DC public zoo,
reproduced on the metro cards

because its image is innocuous
and without a sense of symbol.

Notes

Epigraph taken from *Tom Jones* or *The History of Tom Jones: A Foundling*, 1749: Part I, Book II, Chapter iv, called, "Containing one of the most bloody battles, or rather duels, that were ever recorded in domestic history."

p. 35—"The Extent of the Land" refers to the tradition of the covenant of the plains of Moab.

p. 38—The opening lines are based on an ancient East Indian fable, sometimes called "How the Musk Deer Got Fooled," told to me first by Dale Asreal as part of a talk given on retreat at Shambhala Mountain Center in 2009.

p. 46—The opening lines taken from W.S. Graham's "Proem" from the book *Aimed at Nobody: Poems and Notebooks*, 1993.

p. 49—Harold Hayes was born in 1926 in Elkin, NC. He moved to Winston-Salem, North Carolina when he was eleven years old, and later attended Wake Forest College in Wake Forest, North Carolina, graduating in 1948 just before the college moved to its current location in Winston-Salem. Hayes famously edited *Esquire* from 1963-1974, curating the new journalism movement, shepherding the likes of Norman Mailer, Gore Vidal, Susan Sontag, Nora Ephron and many others. He also wrote a posthumously published biography of Dian Fossey that was the basis for the 1988 film *Gorillas in the Mist*. He died in 1989 in Los Angeles. The poems in part three are an imaginative biography of his time in Winston-Salem and Wake Forest.

p. 51—*Exultet Rolls* are solemn hymns, likely originating in Southern Italy in the fourth century, sung at the blessing of the Easter Candle during the Easter Vigil, now commonly called the *Exultet*.

p. 51—A.R. Ammons attended Wake Forest College at the same time as Harold Hayes, graduating a year later in 1949.

p. 53—"Bath qol" is Hebrew for "daughter of a voice," the term used for the voice of God by the rabbis; in the NT the heavenly voice at the baptism (Mark 1: 11) and transfiguration (Mark 9: 7) of Jesus.

p. 53— "A sound of sheer silence" from 1 Kings c 19 v 12, NRSV.

p. 57—The mural referenced is called "Tapestry of Tobacco" and can be found in the lobby (not the cafeteria) of the Reynolds Building in downtown Winston-Salem, recently vacant, though there are plans to repurpose the building as an upscale hotel. It was created by Dennis Abbe of New York. The Reynolds Building, a design inspiration for the later Empire State Building, was designed by Shreve and Lamb. It was built in 1929 (before the New Deal, an anachronism in the poem) and now stands vacant. The story of the dyed chicks was told to me by my mother, Nancy Little Ekstrand.

p. 59—A hedonic tone assessment is a process of scaling odors in terms of their pleasantness. Sometimes referred to as an *offensiveness* measure. In psychology, the hedonic tone is a way of scaling the pleasantness of emotions, especially in Victor Johnson's Hedonic Tone Theory, also called "valence."

p. 59—Harold Hayes' father served as the pastor at New Hope Baptist Church in Purlear for a time, and was prominent in the Southern Baptist church in NC. Harold Hayes' older brother is named James. This poem takes place before Harold's birth.

p. 69—"Newfangled" from the middle English, "fangled," meaning "to take up" or "caught-up," or later "fangled" could mean something like bobbles, crochets or foppery in fashion, so it would mean "new-fashioned," contemptuously. This later definition is likely the result of a misinterpretation of the earlier definition. The explanation provided in the poem is invented.

p. 71—"When Life Was Full, There Was No History" is a title taken from Thomas Merton's translations of Chuang Tzu called *The Way of Chuang Tzu* published by New Directions.

p. 72—"We haven't fully begun yet to live by the shifts, last century, in the quantum understandings of time and space" is taken from a web interview I conducted for *Gulf Coast: A Journal of Literature and Fine Arts* with Stephanie Strickland called "Elsewheres and In-betweens."

p. 74—"All things from heaven are of like form and come 'round in a circle" is taken from Marcus Aurelius' *Meditations*, Book Two.

p. 74—A reference to the painting *A Philosopher Lecturing on the Orrery* by Joseph Wright of Derby, ca. 1766.

p. 75—"The Myth of the Bird in the Hall" is an ancient Anglo-Saxon parable about the mystery and unlikeliness of human birth and death. In it, human life is compared to a bird flying in and then out of the windows of a mead hall: we do not know where the bird came from before it entered the hall, or where it is going when it leaves.

p. 81—In 2007, the last section of "The Wound Dresser" was inscribed above the Dupont Circle Metro Station in Washington, D.C., omitting the parenthetical couplet with which the poem ends. The entire stanza reads, "Thus in silence in dreams' projections, / Returning, resuming, I thread my way through the hospitals, / The hurt and wounded I pacify with soothing hand, / I sit by the restless all the dark night, some are so young, / Some suffer so much, I recall the experience sweet and sad, / (Many a soldier's loving arms about this neck have cross'd and rested, / Many a soldier's kiss dwells on these bearded lips.)"

Perhaps the omission was merely practical, but it is still ironic as Dupont Circle is one of America's famous gay neighborhoods.

p. 81—Revelation c 3 v 16, NRSV.

Eric Ekstrand lives in Winston-Salem, North Carolina, with his husband, Danny, and his father, Ken. He teaches writing at Wake Forest University. He is the recipient of a 2009 Ruth Lilly Fellowship awarded by The Poetry Foundation and graduated from the University of Houston with an MFA in Creative Writing in 2010. He is a former poetry editor of *Gulf Coast: A Journal of Literature and Fine Arts*. His work has appeared in *Poetry*, *jubilat*, *Indiana Review*, *Black Warrior Review*, *Bat City Review*, and elsewhere.

Laodicea by Eric Ekstrand

Cover photo © Jennifer Ray, 2015, courtesy of the photographer

Cover Typefaces: Adobe Caslon Pro and Myriad Pro
Interior Typefaces: Adobe Caslon Pro, ITC Serif Gothic, and Myriad Pro

Cover and interior design by Gillian Olivia Blythe Hamel

Each Omnidawn author participates fully in the design of his or her
book, choosing cover art and approving cover and interior design.
Omnidawn strives to create books that align with each author's vision.

Offset printed in the United States
by Edwards Brothers Malloy, Ann Arbor, Michigan
On 55# Enviro Natural 100% Recycled 100% PCW
Acid Free Archival Quality FSC Certified Paper
with Rainbow FSC Certified Colored End Papers

Publication of this book was made possible in part by gifts from:
Robin & Curt Caton
Deborah Klang Smith

Omnidawn Publishing
Richmond, California
2015
Rusty Morrison & Ken Keegan, Senior Editors & Publishers
Gillian Olivia Blythe Hamel, Managing Editor, Book Designer,
& OmniVerse Managing Editor
Sharon Zetter, Poetry Editor, Grant Writer & Book Designer
Cassandra Smith, Poetry Editor & Book Designer
Peter Burghardt, Poetry Editor & Book Designer
Melissa Burke, Marketing Manager & Poetry Editor
Liza Flum, Poetry Editor & Social Media
Juliana Paslay, Fiction Editor & Bookstore Outreach Manager
Gail Aronson, Fiction Editor
RJ Ingram, Poetry Editor & Social Media
Josie Gallup, Feature Writer
Sheila Sumner, Feature Writer
Kevin Peters, Warehouse Manager